Essence of Zen

By

Karlo T. G.

*Source of the three Buddhist images in pgs. 3-5:

http://www.tsemrinpoche.com/tsem-tulku-rinpoche/downloads/buddha-images.html

ISBN-13:
978-1503356276
ISBN-10:
1503356272

This book is dedicated for the entire world.

May everyone find inner peace.

May everyone remember that the true state of humanity is being happy.

May everyone become a Buddha.

ཨོཾ་མུ་ནེ་མུ་ནེ་མ་ཧཱ་མུ་ནེ་ཡེ་སྭཱ་ཧཱ།

ཨོཾ་ཏུ་རེ་ཏུ་ཏུ་རེ་ཏུ་རེ་མ་མ་ཨཱ་ཡུཿ་པུཎྱེ་ཛྙཱ་ན་པུཥྚིཾ་ཀུ་རུ་སྭཱ་ཧཱ།

Index

Introduction................................ *7*

What Does The Word Zen Mean?................................ *8*

What is Enlightenment?...................... *9*

Zen Dialogues................................ *11*

Transcendental Quotes and Sayings................................ *28*

Meditation................................ *33*

Applying Meditation In Your Life................................ *38*

Uniqueness & Perfection................ *41*

Zen Stories................................ *45*

Zen Poetry................................ *74*

Introduction

This book is a very simple book, like the essence of Zen. What is the essence of Zen? Well, it cannot be described... The only way to truly understand and "taste" the essence of Zen is to meditate... sit and meditate... and sit... and meditate... and you will eventually "taste the apple of Zen", once that happens, then will know its essence not through the mind, but through your whole being.

The purpose of this book is to simply bridge a glimpse of this essence, and not just that, but also observations, understandings, and wisdom that come as you walk life with the awareness of this essence. So as you read this book, try not to grasp the words, but "taste" the words instead. Just feel the soundless sound, the space between the words, the juice, the taste, the essence. With that being said! May this book be a fun book to read! Enjoy! Kanpai! (Kanpai is the Japanese word for cheers).

What Does The Word Zen Mean?

The word Zen comes from the Sanskrit word Dhyana, which means "meditation". Now when I say Zen, I am not referring to Zen Buddhism. Like mentioned before, in this book we will not focus on the tradition and history of Zen Buddhism, we will focus on the "essence" of Zen, in other words the essence of meditation, not Buddhism. Meditation does not belong to Buddhism, Taoism, Hinduism, or anyone in particular.

Meditation is Universal, and you do not need to be a Buddhist, or change your religion in order to practice it. Anyone can practice Zen, and you do not need a master or a guru to do so. It is good to have the guidance of a master or guru, but it is not a "MUST" to have one in order to practice Zen.

What is Enlightenment?

Now, let us begin this journey by clearing common misunderstandings about enlightenment. Most people think that enlightenment is hard to reach or unreachable, and that it takes thousands of lifetimes to become enlightenment. Some people think that enlightenment means to know all the answers in life, and to have supernatural or extreme metaphysical abilities. Well, enlightenment has nothing to do with that. Enlightenment is simply realizing and becoming aware of whom you truly are, and as you become aware of your "True Self" or "Original Self", you become a Buddha. The word Buddha means "one who is awake (awake and aware of one's own true self)".

Siddhartha (The one who became enlightened under a tree), chose to be called Buddha because he knew that he woke up to the truth, the truth of who he truly was. He saw his "Original Self", which is the source of his being. By being aware of this, he also understood that the source of his being was also the source of the entire universe.

Enlightenment is something that happens, just like when you wake up in the morning, you just wake up when your body has rested enough. In order for enlightenment to happen, one must water and nurture one's own awareness, so that when it is ripe enough or sensitive enough... It happens! All on its own without forcing it! You wake up and you become aware of your "Original Self", in other words you are enlightened.

Zen Dialogues

These dialogues are written differently than what most people are used to reading. They are written in a simple way, and go straight to the point. But, what matters most is the essence they carry, not the words or the way they are written. Enjoy! Kanpai!

Zen Dialogue #1:

A student approached his Zen master and asked:

-**Student:** Teacher, what is the ultimate teaching? What is the ultimate truth?

The Teacher remained silent.

-**Student:** Did you not hear my question?
-**Master:** Did you not hear my answer?

Zen Dialogue #2:

A Zen monk was sitting still in a park. A man came close to him and began to speak to him:

-Man: Are you a monk?

-Monk: Yes I am

-Man: Do you believe in God?

-Monk: What God?

-Man: You don't know God? He is the source of everything! He is the one who created everything!

-Monk: Hmm... Then who created him?

-Man: Oh… Uh... he created himself!

-Monk: What was before him? Before he created himself?

-Man: Uh… hmm... nothing? I guess...

-Monk: Behold! The true source of everything... where everything comes from...

The man sat quietly without saying a word, contemplating on his conversation with the monk.

Zen Dialogue #3:

There was a Zen master walking down the road and he heard a woman screaming:

-**Woman:** God will save you! God forgives everyone! He forgives unconditionally! He is the most Compassionate! God can save you from your sins! Because He loves you all!

The Zen master passed by and the woman started speaking to him:

-**Woman:** God will save you!

-**Master:** From what?

-**Woman:** From your sins!

-**Master:** What is a sin?

-**Woman:** When you do bad things!

-**Master:** What is bad?

-**Woman:** Well... like having sex with a woman!

-**Master:** What happens if I do it?

-**Woman:** Then you must confess you sin to God!

-**Master:** And what happens if I don't confess?

-Woman: Then God will punish you!

-Master: Didn't you say that your God forgives everyone? Didn't you say he forgives unconditionally? He is compassionate and loves us all, but he punishes if you do not confess?

-Woman: He forgives if you confess!

-Master: Then your God does not forgive everyone, because he only forgives to those who confess, what about those who don't? This is not unconditional forgiveness...

The woman was shocked. She could not answer to what the Zen master said. But, she continued:

-Woman: Oh yea? Then who is your Savior!?

-Master: No one... I do not give someone else the power to save me from my own garbage, or give someone else the responsibility to take care of my own garbage... I face my dump head on and take responsibility for my life. This means... I choose how I want to live, and I am responsible for what happens in my life.

The lady remained silent as the Zen master walked away.

Zen Dialogue #4:

A Zen master was walking down a village, and then a man came up to him and asked:

-**Man:** Hi what is your name?

-**Master:** What is your name?

-**Man:** I asked you first

-**Master:** I asked you second

-**Man:** Yes! So who are you?

-**Master:** Who am I? Who are you?

-**Man:** Forget it!

-**Master:** Nice to meet you Mr. Forget it! He he he!

Zen Dialogue #5:

A Zen master and his student were having a conversation, and the student asked:

-**Student:** I heard you say that true happiness comes from within, and that only seeking happiness externally causes suffering. Why is that?

-**Master:** Throughout a year, spring becomes summer, summer becomes fall, and fall becomes winter. What happens to each of the seasons as the year goes on?

-**Student:** They change.

-**Master:** Yes, and as they change you can see that each season does not last forever, they are constantly transforming. This is what we call impermanence. Tell me... how can this relate to everything in the external world we live in?

-**Student:** Hmm... Everything is changing... and... Therefore, everything is impermanent?

-**Master:** He he! Exactly! So, since the external is impermanent, external happiness is also impermanent.

-**Student:** Hmm...

-**Master:** If you are happy because you have a lot of money, then when you lose all that money, you lose your happiness too, because the source of that happiness was money, and money is external.

-**Student:** OH! Now I get it! So that is why if I am happy within, without my happiness depending on having a lot of money, then I will be happy with or without having a lot of money!

-**Master:** He he! You got it! And that is one example of many.

They both left to the meditation hall.

Zen Dialogue #6:

A man came to a Zen master and said:

-**Man:** I need your help!

-**Master:** Hmm...

-**Man:** See... I got slapped by a girl!

-**Master:** Hmm...

-**Man:** I know right! Why did she do that?! All did was asked how much she weighs...

-**Master:** Hmm...

-**Man:** And so I yelled at her!

-**Master:** Hmm…

-**Man:** I know... but I feel kind of bad for her...

-**Master:** Hmm...

-**Man:** Yea, I should probably talk to her. Thank you Zen master!

-**Master:** For what?

Zen Dialogue #7:

A Zen master walked into a room. A man approached him and asked:

-**Man:** Hi, who are you?

-**Master:** I am

-**Man:** You are…?

-**Master:** Yes, I am

-**Man:** You are what!?

-**Master:** No, not what, but who...

-Man: That is what I asked from the start!! Who are you?!

-Master: I am... Ha ha ha!

-Man: ....

Zen Dialogue #8:

Inside a Buddhist temple, a Zen master was instructing a man and asked him:

-Master: Who are you?

-Man: I am Tom

-Master: I did not ask what your name is, I asked who are you?

-Man: Well, I am a Doctor

-Master: That is not you, that is your job, not you... who are you?

-Man: I am a nice guy and I like to play basketball...

-Master: That is your hobby, your personality, not who you are...

-Man: uuugh!!!

-Master: Still not you Ha ha!

-Man: I don't know what you want me to say!

-Master: He he! Funny, how such a simple question cannot be answered.

-Man: Who!? Who am I? I already answered! But you keep saying that is not who I am! If what I described is not who I am, then I don't know who I am!

-Master: Good, not knowing who you are is the beginning of realizing who you are...

-Man: My head hurts... And what would you suggest then! What can I do to "realize who I am?"

-Master: Just realize who you are! Ha ha! Wake up!

-Man: Not helping!

-Master: Ha ha ha! Meditate! Detach from what you "think" you are until you realize who you truly are.

Then, you will naturally be who you truly are without even trying.

-Man: But how do I know when I have realized who I truly am?

-Master: Silly man! Ha ha! You will KNOW when you know it! You will have no doubt about it. Like tasting an apple, you KNOW what it tastes like when you taste it!

He he he! Though, this is not something that can be forced, it happens naturally on its own. But once it happens, it will change your life entirely, fore you will see life with new eyes... Wide open!

Zen Dialogue #9:

A Zen student came to his master and asked:

-**Student:** I have been here in the temple for a long time now, and I still do not understand enlightenment, the ultimate goal.

-**Master:** What is there to understand?

-**Student:** What do you mean?

-**Master:** There is the problem!

-**Man:** What? Where?

-**Master:** Nothing! Nowhere! Ha ha ha!

Zen Dialogue #10:

A Zen master was sitting in a desk drinking tea, and then one of his students approached him and asked:

-**Student:** Master... Why is there so much suffering in the world?

-**Master:** Do you think the world is suffering? Or the world is in pain?

-**Student:** What? is the difference?

-**Master:** Suffering is a state of mind, it is an illusion.

-**Student:** I don't get it...

-**Master:** People just don't see things as they are. If you burn your hand because you touched something hot, some people would relate this pain with suffering. But, if you see things as they are, when you burn your hand, you only witness pain but not suffering. Suffering comes from a victimized state of mind, when someone thinks he or she is a victim in his or her life. So, let go of the mind! And your suffering will be gone!

Zen Dialogue #11:

A Zen master asked four of his disciples:

-**Master:** No Leaf falls in the wrong place, what does this tell you?

Then, each of the disciples replied one by one:
-**1st Disciple:** There is no right or wrong, everything is perfect just as it is.
-**2nd Disciple:** Everything happens for a reason.
-**3rd Disciple:** Everything just is...
-**4th Disciple:** No Leaf falls in the wrong place...

Then, the master said to the first disciple:
-**Master:** I admire your transcendence of duality.

He said to the second disciple:
-**Master:** I admire your recognition of cause and effect.

To the third disciple he said:
-**Master:** I admire your simplicity.

Finally, he spoke to the last disciple:

-**Master:** I admire and bow to you… fore you see things as they are.

Zen Dialogue #12:

A man asked a Zen master:

-**Man:** Is there good and bad? Is there right and wrong?

-**Master:** There is no good or bad, and there is no right or wrong. There is just what is. Good and bad, right and wrong, are all illusions from the mind.

-**Man:** But how? I don't get it?

-**Master:** Well, what you see as good, another person could see it as bad. What you believe is bad, another person can believe it is good. What you think is right, others may think that what you think is wrong, and so on... It is all about perception. This is the game of duality.

-**Man:** How can one get out of this game of duality?

-**Master:** Drop you mental perceptions, and see things as they are. If you hit someone, it is not right and it is not wrong, it is just what it is... you just hit someone.

Now just because there is no good or bad, it does not mean that the person you hit will not react to what you did to him or her. He or she could hit you back, run away, or forgive you. There are infinite possibilities as to how one can react when you hit them... If you understand this, then you have stepped out of duality.

Zen Dialogue #13:

A Zen student went up to his master and asked:

-Student: Master, can you teach me about cause and effect?

The Master flicked the student in the nose.

-Student: Owww!

-Master: He he he! There you go, cause; flick in the nose, effect; Owww! Ha ha ha!

Zen Dialogue #14:

A Zen Master was giving a lecture:

-Master: Emptiness is the base of it all. Just as silence is the base of a song, and the space between the notes determines the length and rhythm of a song. The blank canvas is the base of one's painting. The space between words is what allows one to read a book, a sentence, or any writing with ease. The emptiness of a bowl is what allows one to put food there. The emptiness of a room is what allows one to live there. The emptiness of void is what allows the universe to grow infinitely with infinite possibilities...

-Student: It is like a representation of the Yin and Yang... but in a very subtle way...

-Master: Indeed! Nothing yet everything. The absolute and relative realities are one. I call this "The Primordial Yin and Yang".

Zen Dialogue #15:

Two monks were having a blast together in a farm. They were standing outside and admiring the animals. They heard a dog barking and the 1st monk said:

1st Monk: Ha ha ha that dog reminds me... Does the dog have the Buddha Nature?

2nd Monk: Ha Ha! That saying is so outdated! How about a joke? Here... What did one Zen master cow say to the other Zen master cow?

1st Monk: Oh! Oh! I got it.... MU!!!!!!

And both Monks started laughing.

Transcendental Quotes and Sayings

There is nothing like a little dose of classic, well known quotes and sayings from different kinds of masters. Some may not be specifically Zen, but they share the same transcendental essence of Zen. Enjoy! Kanpai!

"If you are unable to find the truth right where you are, where else do you expect to find it?"

-Dogen Zenji

"Do not seek to follow the footsteps of the wise; seek what they sought."

-Basho

"In the end these things matter most; how well did you love? How fully did you live? How deeply did you let go?"

-Buddha

"To study Buddhism is to study ourselves. To study ourselves is to forget ourselves."

-Dogen Zenji

"Walking is Zen, sitting is Zen."

-Daishi

"Nature does not hurry, yet everything is accomplished."

-Lao Tzu

"A flower falls, even though we love it; and a weed grows, even though we do not love it."

-Dogen Zenji

"Before enlightenment; chop wood, carry water. After enlightenment; chop wood, carry water."

-Buddha

"Silence is a source of Great Strength."

-Lao Tzu

"Whether talking or remaining silent, moving or standing quiet, the Essence itself is ever at ease."

-Daishi

"Every day is a journey, and the journey itself is home."

-Basho

"Peace comes from within. Do not seek it externally."

-Buddha

"If you want to walk the way of Buddhas and Zen masters, then expect nothing, seek nothing, and grasp nothing."

-Dogen Zenji

"If your compassion does not include yourself, it is incomplete."

-Buddha

"Stop thinking, and end your problems."

-Lao Tzu

"To enter the Buddha Way is to stop discriminating between good and bad, and to cast aside the mind that says this is good and that is bad."

-Dogen Zenji

"Pain is certain, suffering is optional."

-Buddha

"Flowers in spring, autumn's moon, summer's breeze, and winter's snow. If your mind isn't clouded by unnecessary things, this is the best season of your life."

-Wu-men

"If you use your mind to study reality, you won't understand either your mind or reality. If you study reality without using your mind, you'll understand both."

-Bodhidharma

"Nothing can be gained by extensive study and wide reading. Give them up immediately."

-Dogen Zenji

"Sitting quietly, doing nothing, spring comes, and the grass grows by itself."

-Basho

"If you are depressed you are living in the past.

If you are worried you are living in the future.

If you are at ease you are living in the present."

-Lao Tzu

"Old pond... frogs jumps in... sound of water."

-Basho

As you can see, these quotes contain the same taste. Different words from different masters to transmit the same essence.

Meditation

If one meditates, this path will lead towards self realization. To understand and experience what the Buddhas and ancient ones talked about, one must meditate. It cannot be grasped intellectually. The mind cannot understand transcendental wisdom, because this wisdom goes beyond the intellectual mind. Transcendental wisdom is too simple for the mind to comprehend, but the heart is a different story.

Those who are Buddhas try to talk about and describe what they have "tasted", but they know that what they talk about is not even close to fully describe the "taste". It is like when someone loves another person so much that just saying "I love you" is not enough to describe the love they feel, but it helps to bridge a glimpse of the essence that is being felt. Same thing goes with enlightenment, you feel it, but talking about isn't enough to describe it at all.

Now, when one begins to practice meditation, the mind becomes afraid and starts to behave more and more like a separate entity of its own. When you start meditating, the mind starts to shoot at you with garbage, and it will seem like it's doing anything it can to prevent you from transcending it and cultivate awareness. It wants you to keep engaging with it, so you can feed it with more energy and add on to its momentum of thoughts. This is the temptation of the mind; it comes up with beautiful, divine, demonic, sad, threatening, clever, exciting, or fearful thoughts to tempt you so that you engage with it and play its game. The mind knows that when you meditate, the mind will lose its power over you and dissolve! Then the monkey business is over!

The key here as you meditate is to not identify with anything, just simply be the observer and witness all thoughts and sensations without grasping them. As you do this, the mind will slowly dissolve and lose its momentum on its own. It is like a big puddle with lots of dirt and ripples. By just observing the puddle without doing anything, you will eventually see that dirt settles at the bottom and the ripples fade away on their own, allowing you to see through the puddle clearly. This is what you do in meditation; letting all of the ripples of the mind fade away, letting the mental garbage settle at the bottom, and as a result your awareness becomes pure, still, and stronger all on its own.

So how does one meditate? Well there are many ways to meditate, but in this book I will introduce a very simple one:

1st: You can sit down on the floor, on a cushion, a chair, your bed, or wherever you feel comfortable. Then, you can sit crossing your legs in the most comfortable position for you. It is not necessary to cross your legs like a guru, with your legs all twisted in what they call "the full lotus position". If you are sitting in a chair, just sit up straight and let your feet touch the ground. Wherever you sit, make sure that you back is straight.

2nd: Put your left hand below your right hand and in front of your navel, with both thumbs touching each other. In traditional Zen Buddhism, they put their left hand on top and right hand below, but you can do whichever makes you feel more comfortable. Make sure that your tongue touching the roof of your mouth, right behind your front teeth. Your eyes can remain slightly open and looking at the floor just a few feet away from you, but I recommend you meditate with your eyes closed.

3rd: When you breathe, make sure you are using your abdomen and not your chest. When you inhale, the abdomen must be expanding outward. When you exhale, your abdomen must be going inward towards your spine.

Once you check these three steps, just start meditating by counting your breath. Count how many seconds you inhale and how many seconds you exhale. Make sure your breaths are even; if you inhale 5 seconds, then exhale 5 seconds as well. This is a tool to reduce mental activity, if thoughts arise, just come back to the breath. If you catch yourself thinking about your dirty underwear, just return to your breath and continue counting. Slowly, the mind will lose momentum and you will witness less mental activity. You will notice that you get to a point in which you don't even need to count your breath, you are just deeply present.

In order to start feeling the effects of meditation, I recommend to meditate for at least 10 to 15 min. (or if you like to meditate longer, then meditate for 30 min.), once or twice a day, every day. The key here is consistency. Also, sometimes it's better to do two short meditations than a 2 hour long meditation. What matters most is how deep you meditate, not how long you meditate. Once you are done meditating, do not rush! Take your time and stretch a little, then move slowly so that your energy does not scatter. As one just keeps on meditating, one will suddenly see, feel, and taste what the masters saw, felt, and tasted. One will become aware of one's own true self, and become a Buddha.

Applying Meditation in Your Life

So how do we apply meditation in our daily lives and not just while sitting down? Well, you can start by processing all of the emotions that you feel every day without grasping or repressing them at the moment you feel them, instead of waiting until you sit and meditate in order to process those emotions (though, there is nothing wrong with that). Feel them, but do not identify with them. Be the observer, just like your sitting meditations.

Let´s say that your girlfriend sleeps with two men, and then takes a dump on your bed and leaves a note attached to it saying "I dump you". Now, instead of trying to escape the pain by smoking weed, cigarettes, or drinking alcohol, just process the pain consciously! Observe it! Do not repress it! Smell the dump she took on your bed! Slowly the anger, frustration, and pain will dissolve (maybe not over night, but it does dissolve). As a result, you will heal and remain pure.

This also applies with traumas. You can heal any trauma by processing it consciously through meditation. A trauma is simply unprocessed emotional pain, and if you process it, then the trauma is gone! Just bring the trauma to your conscious awareness, and breathe deeply as you remember your trauma. You can do it slowly, little by little until you process and heal the trauma completely. Again, this is not an overnight process, unless you are very good at doing this... you never know, humans are capable amazing things.

Another way to apply meditation is by simply being in the moment in everything you do in life. Do everything with totality. If you are going to eat a cookie, then eat it without thinking about the past or the future, just let go and enjoy it the cookie in the present moment to the max! Also, instead of counting your breath, just simplify you're your mindset to what you are doing. This means that if you are eating chocolate, within yourself just say "I am eating chocolate" or just "chocolate". If you are walking just repeat within yourself "walking, walking, and walking", this way you are not thinking about anything that is irrelevant to the present moment. This is how you can meditate within your ordinary day without having to sit down and breathe.

Suddenly, you will start to notice that your senses are amplified and more vivid. You could be washing dishes, and all of the sudden you feel a wave of bliss moving right through you. You start to see things as they are, instead of good, bad, right, wrong, divine, or evil. You start to see with your eyes and not with your mind. You go beyond duality.

Uniqueness & Perfection

Now, by going beyond duality we can start to recognize the perfection of life itself. Many people go on looking for perfection, because they think that everything is imperfect. That type of mindset is nonsense. We are all perfect! Life is perfect just as it is! Even chaos is perfectly chaotic and disorder perfectly in disorder. But people cannot see life's perfection, because it is right in front of their eyes hiding in plain sight! They cannot see it because of their complex mindset.

The ego is not satisfied with life´s simplicity and perfection. The ego is the reason why people start looking for perfection elsewhere. They think that being already perfect is too good to be true, because their ego says "No, that's not it! You do not deserve this! This is too simple, it has no value! You have to struggle and work hard for it!" Also, people believe that because life does not go according to their expectations, they think that life is imperfect. But life just is, and it is not taking sides. You have a cup of water filled half way; is the cup half full or half empty?

Now, let´s dig in a little deeper into the subject of perfection. Why is everything and everyone already perfect? Uniqueness! We are all unique; there is not one being, thing, or place in this universe that is the same. Since we are all unique, there is no need to try to be someone else other than being yourself. Because that is a major problem, people compare themselves to others and try to become like someone else that they think is "more perfect".

If for example, someone has a pet dog and a person kills it, and replaces it with another dog of the same breed, is it the same dog? No, the other dog is dead, and the new dog has his or her own unique personality. The owner of the new dog will not be satisfied and will not recognize the perfection and uniqueness of the new dog, if that person compares it to the previous dog, or has expectations for the new dog to behave and play like the previous dog. It is expectations, which blinds us from seeing the perfection of life. Not one thing can be replaced by another. There is not another being like you in this universe.

It is like a garden of blue flowers, they are all blue flowers, but each one is rooted in its own unique place in the garden. Each flower blooms and blossoms at its own pace, and in its own unique way. They may have many things in common; they may look the same, smell the same, or feel the same, but they are not the same. So, if you want to be someone else, you can't! Because he or she is unique, just like that other person cannot be you, because you are unique. You are who you are, and they are who they are.

"Unique" means one of a kind, and since we are all unique, we are all one of a kind. Now you can see the beauty and perfection of everything and everyone, especially your own beauty and perfection. So don't try to be someone else, be who you truly are. Do not try to be your mother, your father, your family, someone famous, or your best friend. You are who you are, and they are who they are. Accept and see yourself as you are. Also, accept and see life as it is, and you will live in bliss.

Zen Stories

These are short Zen stories. They are all fiction, but they are all inspired by true events, experiences, wisdom, and observations in life. Enjoy! Kanpai!

Zen Story #1:

Once, there was a Zen master living in a temple near a small town. He had a few students living with him. One day, one of his students went into the village at night and ran into a criminal, and the criminal tried to kill him. The student managed to get out of the situation alive.

Later on that night, the student arrived at the temple and he was feeling a lot of anger. The student wanted to kill the man for what he tried to do. He decided not to tell anyone what happened. A few days passed after the incident, and he still felt this intense anger. One day, the master passed by the student and was able to sense his anger. The master told his disciple:

"If you keep holding on to that anger, your energy will become poison. It is ok to feel anger, but holding on to it is a different story. What is going on?"

"Master, this criminal wanted to kill me the other day and now I feel very angry. I feel like I want to kill him, or at least make him pay for what he did!" replied the student.

"Let me ask you something, where is this anger coming from? Who is the one who is feeling this anger?" asked the master.

"I am the one feeling this anger, and the anger is coming from within me"

"Very well, so who is responsible for healing this anger?"

"I... I am master..."

"Good, so do not depend on punishing the criminal in order for you to be happy and heal. Do not give him the power for you to heal. What happens if the criminal is never punished and you never see him again? Will you go on poisoning your energy with anger for the rest of your life?"

"No master... But, how can I get rid of this anger? It is very intense!"

"Regardless of how intense it is, just sit and meditate. Feel it, but do not grasp the anger. Slowly it will settle down and you will heal. As you heal, true forgiveness will be born within your heart"

"Thank you master, I shall keep meditating and not escape from what I feel. I hope my anger settles down"

"Do not worry, you will be fine" said the master.

They both left to the meditation hall and started meditating. It was not easy for the student, it took dedication and a strong will to heal. But after some time, the student felt much better and completely healed his anger.

Zen Story #2:

Once, there was a teenager named Zenji that lived in a very nice city next to a beach. He was going out with his best friend Ibuki, and they were both heading towards the beach to have a good time. But then, Zenji became aware that he was not enjoying the moment as much as he wanted, because he was observing his excessive mental activity. He was labeling everything from within; what was good, what was bad, what he liked, what he didn't like, and he saw that he could not be fully in the present moment because of this ongoing labeling and mental activity.

Then, Zenji remembered that he heard someone mention that meditation was good to settle down the mind. Remembering this, he decided to start doing guided meditations. These meditations were about visualizing divine light, and sending love everywhere with elaborated visualizations. But, Zenji did not feel like it was helping, because visualizing was still using the mind, and he said to himself:

"Even if these thoughts are about divine light and are all pretty, it is still the mind, and it does not help me with being fully in the present moment! I have to find a way to get rid of the mind!"

One day, Zenji and Ibuki were walking in the city and pass by a Zen Center. They both looked at each other and went inside. As they went inside, Zenji was curious about the kind of meditation they did, so he asked the Zen master:

"I have a question about the meditation you practice, can this meditation help one get rid of the mind? I have tried to do other kinds of meditations but they stimulate the mind with fancy visualizations"

"Ha ha ha! Well, in Zazen we focus on the breath. We sit and count our breath. Counting our breath is still using the mind, but it helps to reduce mental activity to just the thought of counting our breath. Your mind starts to simplify and settle down. But after a while, you will not need to count your breath. That is what we call Shikantaza, were you meditate without the support of anything, not even counting your breath" replied the Zen master.

"Wow! Really? That is amazing! And for how long do I have to meditate for the mind to settle down?"

"Well, that is up to you. It all depends on how much you are willing to let go. The key here is consistency, meditate every day without exception" said the Zen master.

"I shall meditate every day without exception! Thank you Zen master!"

That same day, the Zen master taught Zenji and Ibuki how to meditate. From that moment on, Zenji and Ibuki began to meditate every day with determination. After about two months they both felt like a totally different person. Finally, Zenji was able to enjoy his life with totality.

He was in the present moment and was able to truly enjoy life´s pleasures. When he ate a cookie, his sense of taste was so amplified and he felt as if it was the first cookie he had ever tasted in his life. When he went to the beach, he was able to feel everything with his whole being, everything felt so vivid; the sand below his feet, the smell of the sea, the wet breeze, and the sound of the waves crashing. He never felt more awake in his life, and felt that he was truly alive now. Ibuki was also meditating, and he felt the same way Zenji did. They were both enjoying their bliss together and having a good time. They saw the world with new eyes.

Zen Story #3

There was a man whose name was Ku. He was in his late twenties and was living in a big city. Ku lived in fear most of his life. This was a fear that came from his mind. Every day, he woke up and the mind was ready to attack and induce fear within him.

His mind threatened him all of the time. When Ku was enjoying something, all of the sudden the mind popped up with a thought that induced fear, and prevented him from enjoying whatever he was enjoying. He didn't do many things that he wanted to do, because the mind would pop up and strike him with fearful thoughts.

One day, Ku was in a beautiful park sitting down, and a Zen master sits next to him. This Zen master was not wearing a robe, he was wearing normal clothes, and his name was Takada. He looked like an ordinary bald man. Before Takada sat next to Ku, he asked:

"Can I join you?"

"Yea sure" said Ku.

"Do you want an apple?" asked Takada while sitting down.

"Sure! Thank you" replied Ku.

They both started talking and getting to know each other. Takada told Ku that he taught meditation at a small Zen Center. Ku was curious, so he asked the Zen master how to meditate. Takada taught him how, and they both started meditated at the park. Ku was having a blast with Takada, and they both decided to meet often and meditate at the park.

After they were done meditating, Ku returned to his home, and Takada to his Zen Center. When Ku got back home, he started having a lot of fear. This time his fear was stronger than ever, he couldn't handle it, and felt like he was going to die. This fear lasted for days. The time came for Ku to meet again with Takada. They both met in the park were they first met. When Takada saw Ku's face, he noticed that he was not well and asked:

"Ku, are you ok?"

Ku started crying and said:

"I can't stand it anymore! I have lived with fear most of my life, and I am sick and tired of the mind telling me what to do, and to threaten me with fear! I don't know what to do anymore!"

"Ku... it´s alright, come and sit with me, let´s meditate"

"Takada I feel like dying! And if I meditate, I will die for sure!"

"I see what the problem is. You have fear within you, and the mind is threatening you with death right now isn't it? Do you think your mind is real?"

"Yes! And it is driving me nuts!" said Ku desperately.

"I can tell you that the mind and it´s threats are not real. Try to find out, challenge the mind by meditating, and you will see that the fear is not real"

"Ok… I will try" replied Ku with hesitation.

"Feel the fear throughout your body, but do not grasp this fear. Whatever happens within you, just keep meditating and focus on your breath, no matter how intense your fear gets. Trust me, it will all turn out just fine"

"Ok… I trust you Takada".

So they both started to meditate. Ku started to see images he did not like. He felt that if he continued he was going to die. But, he remembered what Takada told him, to just keep meditating and focus on the breath. Ku kept feeling that he was going to die, and this feeling became stronger and stronger. It came to a point where his arms started shaking because of the fear.

Then, suddenly he felt like he just dropped a backpack full of stones to the ground. His shoulders felt lighter, he stopped shaking, and felt at ease. He witnessed how the fear went away, as if it blew up and dissolved. He also felt as if he was flowing smoothly down a river like a leaf. When they finished meditating, Ku looked straight into Takada's eyes and said:

"Takada! I feel... I feel good... it is strange..."

"Ha ha! You have transcended your fear and your mind! Listen, a threat can only affect you if you accept it. The mind is like a hologram, it cannot hurt you. Even if it pulls out a knife, it cannot cut you! It is a hologram! Fear is what the mind uses to try to control you. When the mind pulls out a knife at you, and you think the knife is real, then that is when the mind starts to manipulate you. But, if you know it is not real and you do not listen to the mind, then it cannot hurt you or manipulate you. You saw it yourself! You saw that all of these threatening thoughts and feelings that the mind induces are false and hollow illusions. You did not die my friend! It was not your death! It was your mind's death."

When Ku heard him say that, he immediately resonated with what he said, and tears came out of his eyes. But, these tears were of happiness and relief. He then felt so good that he started to laugh, and Takada laughed with him. Takada knew what Ku was going through, because he went through the same thing years ago. Ku kept laughing, because he felt so good when he realized that the mind was just playing games with him, and that all of his fears were illusions. For the first time ever, Ku was able to enjoy his life without letting fear get in the way.

Zen Story #4:

A guy named John had a beautiful girlfriend, and he loved her so much, but was not fully conscious of how much he truly loved his girlfriend. Her name was Andrea, and she was very kind and joyful. John had difficulty being in the moment though. He was always worried about work, what he was going to do next, where he was going to end up, and always thinking about the future.

He wanted to do so many things with her girlfriend. He was constantly planning what he was going to in the future with Andrea. John was so preoccupied with his plans, that he had very little time to spend with Andrea. When they were together, he did not pay attention to Andrea very much, because he was thinking about their future plans. Andrea could sense his distance, and that he was not truly there with her. She heard John talk about what they were going to do, but what she truly wanted was just for him to enjoy the moment with her, just cuddling was enough to make her happy. But, John never had a clue of what Andrea was feeling.

John had a best friend named Tom. They were both like brothers. Tom has been practicing meditation for a while. John loved talking to Tom about what he was going to do with his girlfriend. But, one day Tom asked John:

"Ok man... you have told me what you are going to do with her in the future many times. But, what have you done with her now? Are you enjoying time with her now? I ask you this because you seem too preoccupied with the future"

"What? How can you say that? Of course I will enjoy my time with her, but once we begin our plans! Right now I can´t... because I need to focus on the plans" said John, and Tom just remained silent.

One day John was sitting down at his desk. It was the afternoon, and Andrea was not back from work yet. John was so tired that he fell asleep at his desk. When he woke up, he noticed that Andrea was not home yet. It was night time already. Then, John gets a call from Tom saying:

"John! It's about Andrea! She's in trouble!"

"What? What are you talking about?" asked John freaked out.

"Turn on the television news man! She got into a car accident!"

"Oh no!" said John shaking.

He turned on the news and saw Andrea´s body stuck inside the car. John panicked and went to the hospital where she was taken. When John arrived to the room where she was being treated, he took her hand and started crying. Then, Tom arrived where John was with Andrea.

After a few minutes, Andrea died. John freaked out and cried even more. All of the sudden, John's plans for their future was worthless, he was not going to be able to enjoy anything with her anymore. The time he could have enjoyed with her was wasted on his worthless plans. Then, Tom looked into Johns eyes and said:

"Sometimes we do not know how much we truly love someone, or recognize the value of what we have right in front of our eyes, until we lose them. John! There is no past, and there is no future! There is only the present moment! So wake up! Wake up!"

Suddenly, John woke up. He woke up at his desk were he fell asleep in the afternoon. He was sweating and breathing very fast. Then, Andrea came inside the house. John was shocked to see Andrea alive, and was relieved that she was ok. He looked at Andrea and started crying:

"Andrea! Oh man! I am happy to see you!"

"What is going on? Are you ok? What happened?" asked Andrea shocked.

"It does not matter what happened or what will happen! What matters most is that we are here together. I love you so much Andrea!"

"I love you too John!" she said overwhelmed.

"Listen Andrea, forget about the future plans, I just want to enjoy my time with you right here, right now"

When Andrea heard this, she was surprised and excited. They both had a real blast for the first time in a while. John visited Tom afterwards. He told him about his terrible nightmare. Tom just laughed and said:

"Well! I am glad you learned how to enjoy what you have in this moment through a dream, and not through an actual accident in your life. That's some pretty trippy stuff man!" and they both started laughing.

John was finally not so preoccupied with the future, and was able to enjoy the present moment. He realized that any day it could all be gone, and that it is better to have enjoyed it, than to lose it all and regret to not have enjoyed anything at all.

Zen Story #5:

Tenzin was a young Tibetan man, and he was an explorer. He loved to travel the world and to see nature's beauty. But he always felt a rush to get to the next place. As he was traveling towards his destinations, he worried more about reaching his destinations rather than enjoying the journey itself. As a result, when he got to his destinations, he was not as satisfied as he thought he would be, so he looked for a different place to travel.

One day, he decided to go hiking in Japan. As he was hiking, he saw a Zen monk sitting down next to a fire, having a cup of tea. Tenzin walked up to the Zen monk and said:

"Hi, my name is Tenzin. Can I join you?"

"Nice to meet you Tenzin! My name is Aiki, and you are more than welcome to join me" replied the Zen Monk.

They both sat down and had a cup of tea together, and started having a conversation:

"I have been traveling for some time now. I have visited many places, and I still have many more destinations to go to. What about you? Do you have a destination?" asked Tenzin.

"Ha ha! No, I have nowhere to go. My destination is the journey itself. This way, wherever I go is where I am meant to be. Wherever I go, I enjoy with totality! here and now is my destination."

Suddenly Tenzin resonated with what he said, and inspired him to join the Zen monk on his journey without worrying about a destination. He was always so preoccupied about arriving at his destinations, that he was getting tired of that, because it did not allow him to enjoy the journey and where he was at the moment.

Tenzin loved the idea of not knowing where to go, and to just go with the flow. He was together with this Zen monk for a while, and the monk taught him many things. One day he was sitting in a very high cliff with the Zen monk, and Tenzin said in a very peaceful voice:

"It does not matter where I am… there is no better place… no better destination… than being in the present moment".

Zen Story #6:

There was a very powerful Zen master whose name was Kanjiro. He used to be the head monk of a Zen Monastery. Now, he has decided to apply his wisdom in the city. He had a friend whose name was Sarah. She was very beautiful, and loved to practice meditation. She had a best friend whose name was Steven.

Sarah and Steven knew each other for a long time now. But as time went by, Steven got very arrogant. He became very materialistic and his ego was very big. Sarah cared about him very much so he asked Kanjiro for his help. Kanjiro accepted to help Sarah and dissolve Steven's ego.

One night, Sarah was having a party at her house because it was her birthday. So she invited Kanjiro, Steven, and many other friends. They were all sitting down having diner, and Steven was talking and saying:

"I have traveled to many places all over the world. I have a job that pays very well, so I have a lot of money to do almost anything I want. I am very well known in many places, and I am very popular. I have done many great accomplishments"

"Hmm... you say I too much... I am, I am, and I am... But, who are you really?" Kanjiro said in a straightforward manner, and suddenly everyone became silent.

"Well, I am Steven of course!"

"That is your name, not who you are... So, who are you?"

"I am rich, I have a mansion, a wonderful car, I love to dance, and I love to go swimming"

"That is property you have and what you like to do, not who you are... you think you are a great man?" asked Kanjiro.

"Yes, I am" replied Steven nervously.

"Funny, you think you are such a great man, but you do not even know you truly are"

Steven was not able to answer that and got even more nervous. Suddenly Sarah changed the subject:

"Steven, there is going to be a retreat. It is in a Zen Monastery, and it will be amazing. Would you like to come?"

"I don't know..." said Steven.

"Ha! You are not great enough to go to a simple Zen retreat?" said Kanjiro hurting Steven's ego.

"Of course I am great enough! Sarah I will go with you to this Zen retreat!" replied Steven.

Sarah got really excited. After a couple of days, they both got prepared for the retreat. When they got to the Zen Monastery, Steven freaked out when he saw Kanjiro. He quickly asked Sarah:

"What is Kanjiro doing here?"

"He is hosting this retreat" replied Sarah, and Steven freaked out even more.

Kanjiro was going to talk and guide everyone individually in the retreat, so that the retreat can be a more personalized experience. When it was Steven's turn to talk to Kanjiro, they both sat silently facing each other. Steven got tired of the silence and asked:

"What now?"

"Your task will be to find out who you truly are" said Kanjiro.

"What? Not this again!"

"Now go and sweep the floor outside"

"You want me to sweep the floor?"

"Stop whining and do it, maybe you will find out who you are as sweep the floor"

Steven went to sweeping the floor, but he was very irritated. After a while, Kanjiro was passing by and Steven told him:

"I am tired of doing a poor man's job! I want to do something else!"

"A poor man's job? HA! Your next task is to clean the bathrooms!"

"What? That is not fair!"

"You consider yourself a great man? And you can't handle sweeping the floor or cleaning the bathrooms?

You are a joke!" said Kanjiro with a big smile on his face.

Steven's ego was hurt again. He went on to clean the bathrooms. But before he did, Kanjiro told him one last thing:

"If you do not find out who you truly are by the end of this retreat, you are not a great man at all"

This affected Steven's ego even more, and he got determined to find out. Kanjiro kept making Steven do heavy chores that affected his ego. Every time they got together Kanjiro would ask Steven who he truly was. Every time Steven replied he got the same answer from Kanjiro:

"NOPE, that is not you!"

After a few days in the retreat, Steven was not able to withstand this anymore. He was in his room and he said to himself:

"I am a great man! But I cannot find out who I am?

I feel this intense frustration! I cannot answer Kanjiro's question of who I am! He always says NO! If what I have told him is not who I am, then don't know who I am! I can't think of anything else to say! But, if I tell him that, he is going to think I am an idiot! This is insane! I am tired of doing these lowlife chores as well! Aaah!"

Steven's ego was so hurt he started crying. It's as if he was going crazy. It was just too much for him to handle that he just decided to let go. He looked up at the roof with tears flowing down his cheeks. Steven took a deep breath and said to himself:

"I give up"

When Steven sat down with Kanjiro again, Kanjiro noticed a difference in Steven's presence, and he asked:

"Who are you?"

"I do not know..."

"Finally! A good answer! That is a good sign Steven, you are doing very well"

"What? I do not get it?"

"Steven, you were holding on tightly to your ego. I was being harsh on your ego so that you would detach from it. You are not who you think you are, and not knowing who you are is the first step to finding out who you truly are. Let go and meditate, and you will see"

"It's funny... when you said let go, that is what I feel... I feel like I am in a let go mood... It feels strange..."

"Yes, you are not resisting anymore. Good progress Steven"

Steven got really inspired by this feeling. He felt at ease. He had done so many things in his life, but the experience he had when he gave up, went beyond it all. After the retreat, Steven kept practicing meditation with Sarah. They both got into a romantic relationship with each other. Sarah was really amazed at the sudden change in Steven's presence and way of being. He was no longer arrogant, and they were both supporting each other's spiritual growth.

Zen Story #7:

There was a new age girl whose name was Tina. She was always inspired by the spiritual path. Tina was a part of a Zen meditation group that was hosted by a Zen master named Ananda. Things always happened to Tina that made her angry, sad, or frustrated. But, she always told herself:

"No, I cannot feel these emotions, because they are not pure. I am a pure being and I cannot allow myself to feel these emotions! I must be happy! Always happy!"

Ananda was very sensitive, and his psychic abilities were very developed. He noticed what was going on within Tina. One day, Tina was at the meditation center and she was not feeling well emotionally. She was trying so hard to not feel like that. Ananda saw that Tina was not well and asked her:

"Are you ok?"

"Yes! Of course! Why do you ask?"

"Tina, it is more than obvious that you are not ok. I can see right through you. You think that in order to be a pure being, you cannot feel emotions such as anger, desire, frustration, sadness, etc. You do not allow yourself to feel those emotions so that you do not get dirty energetically. Listen, your energy right now is neither pure nor bright, and it is because you are repressing all of your negative emotions and not allowing them to flow. When you repress your emotions and deny them, the only thing that happens is that they get stuck in your aura and prevent you from being pure, shiny, and happy. As they get stuck in your aura, your aura becomes muddy and you start to attract situations that are of the same frequency of the emotions that are stuck in your aura. That is why you should feel these emotions, let them pass right through you, but do not grasp or identify with them. This way your aura remains pure, because your energy is flowing. As a result, happiness arises naturally without even trying. Now, Tina… Let it all out!"

Tina resonated with this, and immediately started crying. She let it all out. Finally when she let it all out, she felt lighter and much better. Tina thanked Ananda for this very much. She finally let herself feel all of her emotions without repressing them. She observed them without criticizing or judging what she was feeling, and by doing this Tina reached emotional stability. She was finally happy without trying.

Zen Story #8:

There was a man hiking up a mountain. This man came across another man on his way up the mountain. They did not say anything, they just smiled at each other. They both started a fire, and took out their dried tea herbs. One had dried jasmine, and the other had lemongrass. They boiled some water in a metallic container, and served themselves tea.

They were both silent the whole time. The energy and silence they both had around them and within them, was very penetrating. They both were just sitting and drinking their tea. They were listening to the sound of the birds singing, the wind blowing, the fire burning, and they could also feel each other's presence. They could both hear the silence between all of the sounds that were made by nature.

Both men looked at each other, and they both started laughing. When there is so much silence within, one becomes so blissful that laughter just bursts within you. This is what was going on with these two men. So they kept laughing for a while.

The day turned to night, and they both slept right next to the fire. When the dawn came, they were both already awake. Silently, they both bowed down to each other. The Taoist master went up the mountain one way, and the Zen master went the other way.

They both left with smiles on their faces. They knew they were going to meet each other again when they reached the top of the mountain, and once they did, they were going to have another blissful cup of tea together.

Zen Poetry

I would like to end our journey with a little Zen poetry. These are Zen poems I wrote a while back. I hope you all enjoy! Kanpai!

Satori

-

Nothing to do,

Nowhere to go,

Just go with the flow,

By letting go.

-

Nothing to lose,

Nothing to gain,

What is there to attain?

There is nothing to attain...

At last! Awareness!

-

Who?

\-

Nothing,

Yet Everything.

Empty mind,

Yet Aware.

\-

Not here,

Not there,

Yet Everywhere.

\-

Blissful,

And fulfilled.

Yin,

And Yang.

\-

Zen Trees

-

The trees...

Move as the breeze...

Blows...

Gently, softly, as it blows.

-

The trees are.

The trees grow.

The trees are...

In a Zen state.

-

Birds

-

The birds sing,

When they feel like singing.

They do not sing,

When they don't feel like singing.

-

The birds eat,

When they feel like eating.

The birds sleep,

When they feel like sleeping.

-

The birds fly,

When they feel like flying.

The birds flow with ease,

Like a gentle breeze.

-

True State of Humanity

-

Freedom and simplicity,

Long forgotten qualities,

Because of the insanity

Of humanity.

-

But the true state of humanity,

Is not insanity.

The true state of humanity,

Is happiness and simplicity.

-

CPSIA information can be obtained at www.ICGtesting.com
Printed in the USA
LVOW10s1020301015

460432LV00020B/209/P